What Kind of Seed Made You

poems by

Rachael Inciarte

Finishing Line Press
Georgetown, Kentucky

What Kind of Seed Made You

Copyright © 2021 by Rachael Inciarte
ISBN 978-1-64662-689-2 First Edition
All rights reserved under International and Pan-American Copyright Conventions. No part of this book may be reproduced in any manner whatsoever without written permission from the publisher, except in the case of brief quotations embodied in critical articles and reviews.

ACKNOWLEDGMENTS

I am grateful to these publications, in which the following poems originally appeared, sometimes under different titles or alternate versions:

on visiting Joshua Tree while two simultaneous brush fires burn in Thermal, CA ~ *Up The Staircase Quarterly*, Issue #48
mantis ~ *Figure 1, 4.a*
the dog's mouth ~ *Borderlands: Texas Poetry Review*
seismic; things you might not know about desert animals ~ *Thin Air Magazine*
boys on the rock (Venezuela, 2019) ~ *Glass: A Journal of Poetry*
thorns ~ *Ghost Proposal*
childhood ~ *Juked*

Publisher: Leah Huete de Maines
Editor: Christen Kincaid
Cover Art: Alyson Galgano
Author Photo: Himilcon Inciarte
Cover Design: Elizabeth Maines McCleavy

Order online: www.finishinglinepress.com
also available on amazon.com

Author inquiries and mail orders:
Finishing Line Press
PO Box 1626
Georgetown, Kentucky 40324
USA

Table of Contents

on visiting Joshua Tree while two simultaneous brush fires burn in Thermal, CA 1

mantis 2

geode 3

seismic 4

things you might not know about desert animals 5

thorns 6

small fires 8

childhood 9

what he held 10

boys on the rock (Venezuela, 2019) 11

what the water takes 12

the dog's mouth 13

the body 14

the body as a desert tortoise 15

windblown west 16

fortunes 17

a different kind of particle 18

summer seeds 19

Thank You 20

*to my family—
my loves—Himilcon, Leesán, and Lorel;
my mother Debbie, whom I promised my first book
dedication; and to my father Len, my very first and best reader*

on visiting Joshua Tree while two simultaneous brush fires burn in Thermal, CA

there are things in the world which only
grow by luck, by rare rainfall, by
pollen tacked to the wings of white moths

in the high desert I imagined that
anything surviving must be hearty but
not all of us are made as Oaks

some of us are born Joshua Trees, a
tangle of time spent bending to the
will of wind, proving up and ever reaching

consider though—two hundred years to
grow and only twenty minutes to burn
down, no matter what kind of seed made you

mantis

my friend inherited a flower farm
after years of digging up carrots
unearthing root vegetables hidden below
loam tucked into nail beds and her fingertips
stained the colors of a California sunrise

she calls me before her grandmother's burial
beneath the soil of a different coast
today is Día de los Muertos
the ground is already frozen solid and we are
so happy to watch the seasons die

listen to this, she says,
a mantis on my farm stalked a hummingbird
for weeks
I thought she would starve to death
until one day she caught the bird

I ask her what happened next and
she can show me photos of a headless body
wings still intact, tail feathers pointing East
they eat the brains, just that
what happened to the mantis I wonder

she is dead now, of course

geode

after all we learn to harden
our molten ache cools
to becomes stone

then we worry it until it is crystalline
and when it cracks we can show a geode
here is my wound polished and glittering
look how beautiful

someday someone will see it and say "Ah,"
this pain is safe to handle
pick up and set it back down
to forget except occasionally
when it catches the light and winks

seismic

we meter the earth
measure each heave and tremor
not expecting to find that we are rolling
over the belly of a breathing mass
which groans and shudders the way
an old house might cough in the wind

every minute a quake
of another magnitude
is it vertigo or can you feel the fissures?
there are so many places where the ground has worn thin
how will you know your tread has become too heavy
until you've fallen straight through?

things you might not know about desert animals

the kookaburra laughs
because it is better than you
it needs no oasis in the desert
it feels no thirst at all

a chuckwalla can sneeze crystal
salts but you do not
sparkle like mica
winking in the sand

wallabies birth their joeys
no bigger than a bean
painless compared to a human
child tearing free

the mother keeps three children:
one at her hip
one growing at the teat
one in secret

the last is a seed tucked deep in her belly
just in case because she is desert wise
knows nature is not sweet to the weak
knows we are all so easily replaced

thorns

I.

all over the house I find goat head thorns / thistles that sting and with every step I learn to be more cautious than the last / they're carried in on the rubber soles of our shoes or between our toes / picked up around the neighborhood with bits of block chisme / besos served like backhanded compliments / whose husband and hijos did what and / what kind of a mother / I envy the things I knew before my first was even a seed inside my belly / and when my children burst into bloom we pick this home the way a hermit crab chooses a larger shell because it is more / because
there is need

II.

each child is a different latitude and longitude / I have a sand child and a snow child / a wild child and a worried child / my children are honey and rose they have thorny tongues and claws too / both thrashed in my belly like fish before they tasted their beginning breaths / the first he came to me in a dream / I waited for the second as sand passes through the throat of an hourglass / one I raised beneath a white sky / I filled the furnace with wood from a cord made the pyre lit the match myself to keep his toes warm / the other cuts her teeth on dust whipping through the mountains / the Santa Ana winds blow her hair into curls / that do not come through my blood / both will see the sunrise in the morning under my care / who are these creatures made of such dissimilar stuff / a little bit mine and a little more all their own

III.

once I lived inside a hundred year home beside ghosts in the cold North / the land needed nothing from me to blossom / here I can't get the lawn to do more than yellow and die / all I grow are weeds and thorns / so many thorns they are carried inside to fill cracks in the tile / my son asks for the bigger bedroom when we move and I tell him we won't go / he says alright but next time / I wonder if I have broken his compass / warped his true North so that he will never believe in any place he can call home / my daughter is not even two has had at least as many homes / three if you can count the cozy room of her birth

IV.

neither of my thumbs are green so how will I sow these babies raise them from seed / I know there are five things a plant needs: water; sunlight; soil; air; and /   space   / but when is the right time to harvest a child / what kind of mother / I don't know how to grow anything with effort / that won't one day wither and become thorns

small fires

the torched sky is made
of so many small fires
in the mountains, too
there is flame
forging angels from pine
the haloed smoke blows
brittle splinters and ash
once bird nest or bone

but all kinds of things can catch
a mother says to her family,
"let's bake a cake
to burn out the sadness"
she believes the lost acres
won't haunt like ghosts
drawing air from the room
won't smother like a pillow
laid over a face

childhood

listening at keyholes is a childhood problem
is how you discover the monster beneath your bed is
inside the walls

the walls of your childhood home are full of bees full
of cotton soft spider eggs and
the pock marks on your legs are angry like burns

to smoke out the house you burned it
to the studs the spiders escaped hidden
inside the rosebud flesh of your eardrums

you were born with banana skin your father says you
bruise too easily beneath the surface your mother
cannot speak with her lips buttoned shut

what he held

a coin in his hand a rock or bead
my brother held a mystery and screamed

we had to pry the treasure from his fingers
even then he tried curling them back

the way an oyster bites down
protecting its pearl

the hornet was still alive and stinging
while he clutched and cried

I still don't know how he managed
to get ahold of it in the first place

boys on the rock
  (Venezuela, 2019)

see the boys on the rock, browned bodies grabbing
the sunlight, ribcages cupping their guts
holding in hunger

their nails are silver scales, knuckles sharp and fine
wire wraps their fingers like promise rings like promise
tomorrow they might be fed

see their hooks glinting off the water, pins and knives and
if it is true that necessity is the mother of invention then
it is also true that necessity is the mother of orphans

watch the boys how they fix their gaze to the birds
the pelican's beak is a compass rose is an arrow is
a spoonful in an empty mouth

once there were umbrellas on the beach
once these huts had cook fires had things to cook
over the flames smell the echo of hot grease burning on coals

there were whole fish grilled on plates, their eyes scooped out
dressed in tajadas and salsa rosada, the only fish left
are those the boys pull from the ocean scrawny as themselves

see them study the waves a text a bible most holy
water lapping waves, tongues wet with desire and
calling each other like happy gulls

do not misunderstand them only a small part
is hollow, but their eyes are over the horizon
as full as the sea

what the water takes

cold water beaches are not harbors
they are mouths foaming

children baptized in salt water baths
or raised on tide time know this

their eyes are the lighthouses and have seen
how the seafloor is powered in bone dust

understand that the impulse to throw rocks
into the surf and terrorize gulls is fearborn

on these shores pain is barnacle sliced skin
sand kicked into sunsore eyes

all hearts are like sunken ships
waterlogged even before birth

and costal children are periwinkle hiding
soft underbellies beneath exoskeleton

water is our origin it makes sense
to worry the tide might draw us back in

the way we scare when Mama says
'I brought you into this world,
and I can take you out'

the dog's mouth

barking reminds me of Havana
reminds me of the dog asleep in the shade
of watching feral children play happy in the street
throwing rocks and peeling palm fronds as easily
as I might have picked a dandelion

I smiled to see them tread sweetly around her while
beating each other into broken pavement
games unknowable
whooping like the morning roosters
like sidewalk royalty

that was the night our water got cut
we carried bottles home through the moon bathed plaza
glass glittering like stars underfoot
and across our path unmoved
lay the dog

her belly was distended matted fur and
mouth yawning open
inside the gums were rotten
but her jaws had been stuffed with
wilting orchids

when I think of the dog's mangled shape I
imagine instead her chest rising and falling
with each breath returned
or else I remember children with armfuls of flowers
forcing life into a thing already gone

this body

the body is a barometer
I rise and fall within

imagine a glass, imagine a gauge
imagine pressure now

press your fingers to the fissure
to keep the insides in

because maybe you don't know
how things are always trying to leave me

my mind, my pulse
air promised by breath

small spaces are too unfriendly
hidden with barbs and teeth like

my mouth: a small spaces that holds tongue
your mouth: a small space that keeps lies

scatter me instead like handfuls of grave dirt
nothing left untouched

and when you think of me think about
the hollowed bones of a bird

how I have no weight and
no will to stay down

the body as a desert tortoise

empty bowl collecting sand
cracked keratin teacup

abandoned sip of yolk sun
when the golden hour touches me

once I homed a dinosaur
once I was a spine

I can keep a secret
can keep safe a year of water

but I am born too soft
for this world

finished when the ravens come
to raid our nests

tender bellies sliced
between scissor beaks

my organs might have lived
a hundred years more

but my shell will remain
longer without me

pulverized into a fine
and beautiful dust

windblown west

I cut my teeth on icicles
crystallizing overhead like daggers like
the horse-hair sword
and I was Damocles
waiting for the first thaw of Spring

the West wind carves fractals
into the lens of my glasses
from dust, whipped into a halo over the mountains
and when I blow my nose in bed,
black sand wets my tissues

lore claims the Santa Anas
not for those wheat colored strips of map
but for *Satanás*, Satan's own breath
and with skin chapping,
I believe

on the other side of the mountains
bones make for good kindling
this is the kind of wind that starts fires
but I live in *las manos de Dios and
Dios me cuide*

back East, cold water pipes burst in the basement
but here they are buried deep to avoid boiling over
and while I can to search for the oasis
learn to seek shade in the desert
the windmills will point me out

a wind blown thing
a stray leaf swept far from home

fortunes

I learned fortune telling before the end of the world I wanted to know /
which horseman to saddle myself to / who best to drag me on the way
out /

in each palm a lifeline shattered / the holy places defiled with salt and
smoke / we prayed
to every god / raised lambs opened their throats wide
and warm at the altar /

but we couldn't sing for all the coughing / while we burned the herbs
to make us pure / and
when I read our tarot at the final hour /
every card pulled—
a tower

a different kind of particle

I cannot believe we were stars
when I have searched and
there is nothing in me shining so brightly

say we are a different kind of particle
plain flour sifted through fingertips and
baked into birthday cakes

dunes of winking sand
faceted and unmade too often
swept away

we have too much faith in the sky
I am more impressed by the ash
that buried Pompeii beneath its skin

let us be smoke in the lungs
let us be dust in the eyes
and salt in the wound too

let us one day become soil and bone
the roots will hug our splinters long after
stars have lost sight of us

summer seeds

honor the okra
celebrate the summertime crops
trial by fire fruit that grows
on dew and desert wind

praise the date palms digging so deeply
into the scorched earth
finding buried rivers and
drinking their fill

weathering in ways
only they can
with thorns and burrs
buried or blooming in the heat

learn then how to build a thicker skin
how to keep a red heart rooted
safe and whole
and beating

Thank You

I am indebted to Kristian Macaron for her unerring support, and Sonja Vitow for their loving readership. Thank you to Rebecca Podos for their friendship and confidence in my work, and to Mandala White for her encouragement. I am fortunate to be surrounded by a close group of talented writers and friends, and would be remiss if I did not acknowledge them by name: Amanda Hartzell, Holli Downs, Marlena Clark, and Zaynah Qutubudin. Finally, thank you Emma Harris, who inspires poems and occasionally appears in them.

Rachael Inciarte is a New England transplant currently living in California with their husband and their two children. They hold an MFA from Emerson College in Boston, Massachusetts. Their poems have been nominated for the Best of the Net, and appear in such publications as *Juked, Poetry Northwest, Normal School, Radar Poetry*, and others.

What Kind of Seed Made You is their first published chapbook, inspired by life in the desert. Rachael is growing a garden, and it is thriving.

www.ingramcontent.com/pod-product-compliance
Lightning Source LLC
LaVergne TN
LVHW041525070426
835507LV00013B/1816